Dominican Heritage

Celebrating Diversity in My Classroom

By Tamra B. Orr

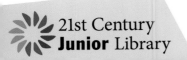

Published in the United States of America by
Cherry Lake Publishing
Ann Arbor, Michigan
www.cherrylakepublishing.com

Reading Adviser: Marla Conn MS, Ed., Literacy specialist, Read-Ability, Inc.

Photo Credits: © Anna Jedynak / Shutterstock Images, cover; © G-Valeriy / Shutterstock Images, 4; © saaton / Shutterstock Images, 6; © GiuseppeCrimeni / Shutterstock Images, 8, 18; © Valeriya Pavlova / Shutterstock Images, 10; © Salvador Aznar / Shutterstock Images, 12; © Lisa F. Young / Shutterstock Images, 14; © Klemzy / Shutterstock Images, 16; © Hiroyuki Saita / Shutterstock Images, 20

Library of Congress Cataloging-in-Publication Data
Name: Orr, Tamra, author.
Title: Dominican heritage / by Tamra B. Orr.
Description: Ann Arbor : Cherry Lake Publishing, 2018. | Series: Celebrating diversity in my classroom | Includes bibliographical
   references and index. | Audience: Grade K to 3.
Identifiers: LCCN 2017035943 | ISBN 9781534107373 (hardcover) | ISBN 9781534109353 (pdf) | ISBN 9781534108363 (pbk.) |
   ISBN 9781534120341 (hosted ebook)
Subjects: LCSH: Dominican Republic—Juvenile literature.
Classification: LCC F1934.2 .O77 2018 | DDC 972.93—dc23
LC record available at https://lccn.loc.gov/2017035943

Cherry Lake Publishing would like to acknowledge the work of The Partnership for 21st Century Skills.
Please visit *www.p21.org* for more information.

Printed in the United States of America
Corporate Graphics

CONTENTS

Many **tourists** visit the Dominican Republic for its pristine beaches.

Dazzling Dominican Republic

The Dominican Republic is an island country. The country is only about the size of two New Hampshires. Yet almost 11 million people live there.

Many people from the Dominican Republic have **emigrated** to other countries. There are almost 1 million **immigrants** from the Dominican Republic in the United States! What is their home country like? Read along to find out!

Santo Domingo is the capital of the Dominican Republic.
It was founded in 1496.

Dime a ver?

Spanish is the main language in the Dominican Republic. There are **slang** terms just like in most American cities. One of the most well-known is *"Dime a ver?"* It means "Tell me so that I can see." But people use it to ask "What's up?"

English is heard in the bigger cities. Sometimes the languages are mixed together. For example, people often ask,

Chess is a popular game in the Dominican Republic.
Learn how to play online or at your library!

"Que lo wha?" Que is Spanish for "what."
Wha stands for the English word "what."
It looks like they're asking "What what?"
But the phrase means "What's going on?"

Ask Questions!

What slang terms do you use? Can you think of phrases that might confuse someone from another country? How about these? "I'm feeling under the weather." "That cost an arm and a leg." "Once in a blue moon."

About 78% of the population in the Dominican Republic is Catholic.

Different Religious Groups

Most of the people from the Dominican Republic are Roman Catholic. This religion was first introduced by Christopher Columbus. The explorer came to the island in the late 15th century.

On the north coast of the country is the small town of Sosua. Most of the island's Jewish people live here. Their families came here after escaping Germany during

Santeria shops sell everything from religious figurines
to charms for good luck.

World War II. Buddhists have also moved onto the island over the last 50 years.

Some Dominicans practice Santeria. The word means "worship of saints." It is a religion that comes from Africa. Charms, herbs, and **potions** are often used in their ceremonies.

Plantains look like bananas, but are less sweet
and taste a bit like potatoes.

Colmados and Chinola

Do you think breakfast is the most important meal? It isn't in the Dominican Republic! The favorite meal is lunch. The most common dish is *la bandera*, or "the flag." It is a plate filled with white rice, beans, fried **plantains**, meats, and vegetables.

A lot of tasty treats are found on the island. *Mangú* is mashed plantains. It's usually served with cheese and bacon.

Tropical fruit is available year round.

Chimichurris are hamburgers piled high with tomatoes and cabbage. People living on the coastline eat a lot of seafood. It's often served with a white sauce made of coconut milk. *Colmados*, or street stores, offer drinks and desserts. Many people enjoy *chinola* (passion fruit juice) on a hot afternoon. Others choose *frio frios*, which is shaved ice with fruit syrups. *Agua de coco* is a drink made from sliced coconuts. It is mixed with sugarcane juice and either mangos, pineapples, oranges, or bananas.

Merengue is also known as *perico ripiao,* which means "ripped parrot."

Music and Water Sports

What happens when you put together a bass guitar, an accordion, a saxophone, a trumpet, and drums? You get a *merengue* band! This type of music is heard all over the Dominican Republic. It is the country's national music. A festival is held each summer to celebrate it. Bands fill the island with exciting music, and people everywhere dance.

Windsurfers rely on the wind to power their boards across the waves.

It is no surprise that so many people visit this country. They come to watch thousands of whales **migrating**. Others dive into the ocean to **snorkel**, surf, or windsurf. Museums keep their doors open until midnight and entry is free.

Look!

Look at this photo of people windsurfing. One of the world's biggest windsurfing contests is held in the Dominican Republic. People come from all over to see if they can win. What would be the hardest part of this type of surfing? What kinds of skills would you need to have?

GLOSSARY

emigrated (EM-ih-grayt-id) left your home country to live in another country

immigrants (IM-ih-gruhnts) people who have moved from one country to another and settled there

migrating (MYE-grayt-ing) moving from one area or climate to another

plantains (PLAN-tinz) fruits similar to bananas

potions (POH-shuhnz) drinks that are supposed to have some kind of power

slang (SLANG) colorful word or group of words that often have a different meaning than their original one

snorkel (SNOR-kuhl) to swim with a mask and tube for breathing

tourists (TOOR-ists) people who visit a place for fun

Spanish Words

agua de coco (AG-wah deh KOH-ko) sliced coconuts with fruit

chimichurris (chim-ee-CHUR-reez) hamburgers with cabbage

chinola (chee-NOH-lah) passion fruit juice

colmados (kohl-MAH-dose) street stores

Dime a ver (DEE-meh ah veh) What's up?

frio frios (FREE-oh FREE-ohz) shaved ice with flavors

la bandera (lah ban-DARE-ah) a common lunch meal

mangu (MAHN-goo) mashed plantains

merengue (meh-RANG-ay) style of Spanish music and dance

Que lo wha? (keh loh wha) What's going on?

FIND OUT MORE

BOOKS

Cantor, Rachel Anne. *Dominican Republic.* New York: Bearport Publishing, 2016.

Sullivan, Laura. *Dominican Republic.* New York: Cavendish Square Publishing, 2017.

Tavares, Matt. *Growing Up Pedro.* Somerville, MA: Candlewick, 2015.

WEBSITES

Ducksters—Dominican Republic
www.ducksters.com/geography/country.php?country=Dominican%20Republic
Find facts about the country's people, geography, language, and more.

Mr. Nussbaum—Dominican Republic for Kids
http://mrnussbaum.com/dominican-republic-for-kids/
Learn lots of facts about the country's people, economy, and government.

INDEX

ABOUT THE AUTHOR

Tamra Orr is the author of hundreds of books for readers of all ages. She graduated from Ball State University, but moved with her husband and four children to Oregon in 2001. She is a full-time author, and when she isn't researching and writing, she writes letters to friends all over the world. Orr enjoys life in the big city of Portland and feels very lucky to be surrounded by so much diversity.